J363.2 STANIFORD
Staniford, Linda,
Police to the rescue around the world
/

TO THE RESCUE!

Police
to the Rescue Around the World

Linda Staniford

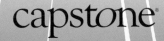

Edited by Linda Staniford
Designed by Steve Mead
Picture research by Eric Gohl
Production by Aileen Taylor
Originated by Capstone Global Library Ltd
Printed and bound in China

19 18 17 16 15
10 9 8 7 6 5 4 3 2 1

Library of Congress Cataloging-in-Publication Data
Cataloging-in-publication information is on file with the Library of Congress.
Written by Linda Staniford
ISBN 978-1-4846-2750-1 (hardcover)
ISBN 978-1-4846-2754-9 (paperback)
ISBN 978-1-4846-2758-7 (eBook PDF)

Acknowledgments
The author and publisher are grateful to the following for permission to reproduce copyright material:
Alamy: Agencja Fotograficzna Caro, 10, 22 (middle), Eric Nathan, 9, ZUMA Press, Inc, 21; AP Photo: Imaginechina, 20, Toby Talbot, 13, 22 (top); Getty Images: Cameron Spencer, 14; iStockphoto: tirc83, 7, Yuri_Arcurs, 5; Newscom: EPA/Massimo Percossi, 17, KRT/Mandi Wright, 19, 22 (bottom), REX/Per Lindgren, 16, ZUMA Press/Taylor Weidman, 15; Shutterstock: AFNR, 11, arindambanerjee, 8, EJMzagsfan, cover, pcruciatti, 4, Phil McDonald, 18, back cover (right), sdecoret, 6, VanderWolf Images, 12, back cover (left)

Design Elements: Shutterstock

Every effort has been made to contact copyright holders of any material reproduced in this book. Any omissions will be rectified in subsequent printings if notice is given to the publisher.

All the Internet addresses (URLs) given in this book were valid at the time of going to press. However, due to the dynamic nature of the Internet, some addresses may have changed, or sites may have changed or ceased to exist since publication. While the author and publisher regret any inconvenience this may cause readers, no responsibility for any such changes can be accepted by either the author or the publisher.

007501RRDS16

Contents

Some words are shown in bold, **like this**. You can find out what they mean by looking in the glossary.

What Do the Police Do?

Police come to the rescue to keep us safe. Around the world, they stop people from breaking laws and committing crimes.

When someone commits a crime, the police try to catch that person. They also help people who have been hurt when a crime is committed.

How Do the Police Keep Us Safe?

Every country in the world has laws. Laws are like rules, and they are meant to keep us safe.

If people break a law, they may cause **damage** or hurt other people. The police make sure that people do not break the laws of the country they live in.

What Do the Police Wear?

Police officers wear a **uniform** with a hat or helmet. They may wear special **body armor** that protects them from **injury**.

In India, where it is often hot, police wear light-colored uniforms with short sleeves. In Russia, where it can be very cold, they wear thick coats and warm hats.

What Do the Police

Police carry a radio so that they can contact each other quickly. They have handcuffs for when they catch a **criminal**.

Some police officers carry weapons. Different countries have different rules about which weapons, such as guns, are allowed. Sometimes police officers have to carry riot shields. These stop them from getting injured by crowds.

How Do the Police Travel?

Police officers often drive specially marked cars and motorcycles. These have loud sirens and flashing lights. They can also ride bikes.

In Russia, it can be very cold and snowy.
Police cannot use cars where there is
deep snow, so they travel by **snowmobile**.

How Do the Police Rescue People?

In Australia, some people live far away from towns and cities. If they get lost or injured, the police use a helicopter to rescue them.

In Nepal, there was a huge **earthquake**. The ground shook and buildings **collapsed**. Police helped rescue people who were trapped underneath the rubble.

What Are Water Police?

In Venice, people travel on **canals** instead of on roads. The police use boats or jet skis to travel to where they are needed.

Police divers search underwater for injured people or **evidence** of crimes. When a big ship was wrecked in the sea near Italy, police divers helped rescue passengers.

Do the Police Use Animals?

The police ride horses at events where there are large crowds of people. The Canadian Mounted Police are famous for using horses in their work.

Dogs have a very good sense of smell. They can even smell weapons in people's bags. This dog is being used to search for weapons at an airport.

Making the World a Safer Place!

Police often visit schools and communities. They talk about how we can stay safe in our homes and on the streets.

The police are very brave people. It is
good to know we can call them if there
is an **emergency**. But it is also important
to know how to keep ourselves safe.

Quiz

Question 1
What kind of transportation do police often use in Russia?
a) snowmobile
b) helicopter
c) horses

Question 2
Which of these would a police officer usually carry?
a) a shopping bag
b) a radio
c) a library book

Question 3
What do the police use dogs for?
a) to find their lunch
b) to keep them company
c) to find hidden weapons at airports

Answers: 1a), 2b), 3c)

Glossary

body armor protective clothing worn to prevent injury to the body

canal human-made waterway

collapse fall down suddenly; buildings often collapse during earthquakes

criminal someone who breaks the law

damage injury or harm

earthquake very strong shaking or trembling of the ground

emergency sudden and dangerous situation that must be handled quickly

evidence information, items, and facts that help prove something is true or false

injury damage to a part of the body

snowmobile vehicle with an engine and skis or runners; snowmobiles travel over snow

uniform special clothes that members of a particular group wear

Find Out More

Books

Bowman, Chris. *Police Officer* (Dangerous Jobs). Minneapolis: Bellwether, 2015.

Chancellor, Deborah. *Police Rescue* (Emergency Vehicles). Mankato, Minn.: Smart Apple Media, 2014.

Oxlade, Chris. *Police Car* (QEB Emergency Vehicles). Irvine, Calif.: QEB, 2010.

Internet sites

Facthound offers a safe, fun way to find Internet sites related to this book. All of the sites on Facthound have been researched by our staff.

Here's all you do:
Visit www.facthound.com
Type in this code: 9781484627501

Index